RIVERS AND RAILS

A MILEPOST GUIDE TO THE THUNDER MOUNTAIN LINE

BY
DIETER LEIPF

Library of Congress Catalog Card
Number 2001 126554

ISBN 0-927022-57-5

Produced by:
Forgotten Rails, Inc.
P. O. Box 1353
Meridian, Idaho 83680-1353

Printed by:
CHJ Publishing
1103 West Main
Middleton, Idaho 83644

This book is dedicated
to the memory of my parents, who always encouraged my
interest in history and railroads.

Table of Contents

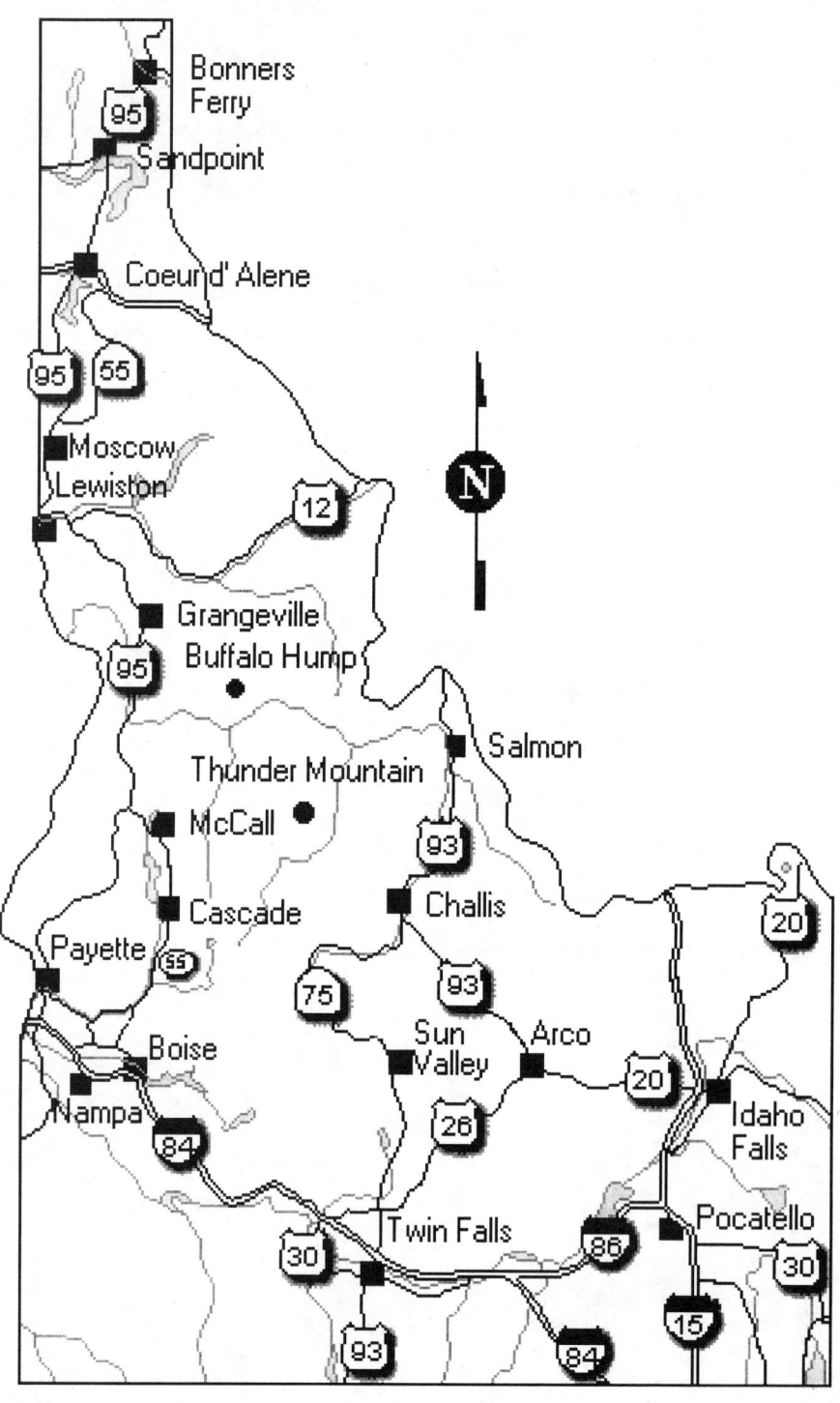

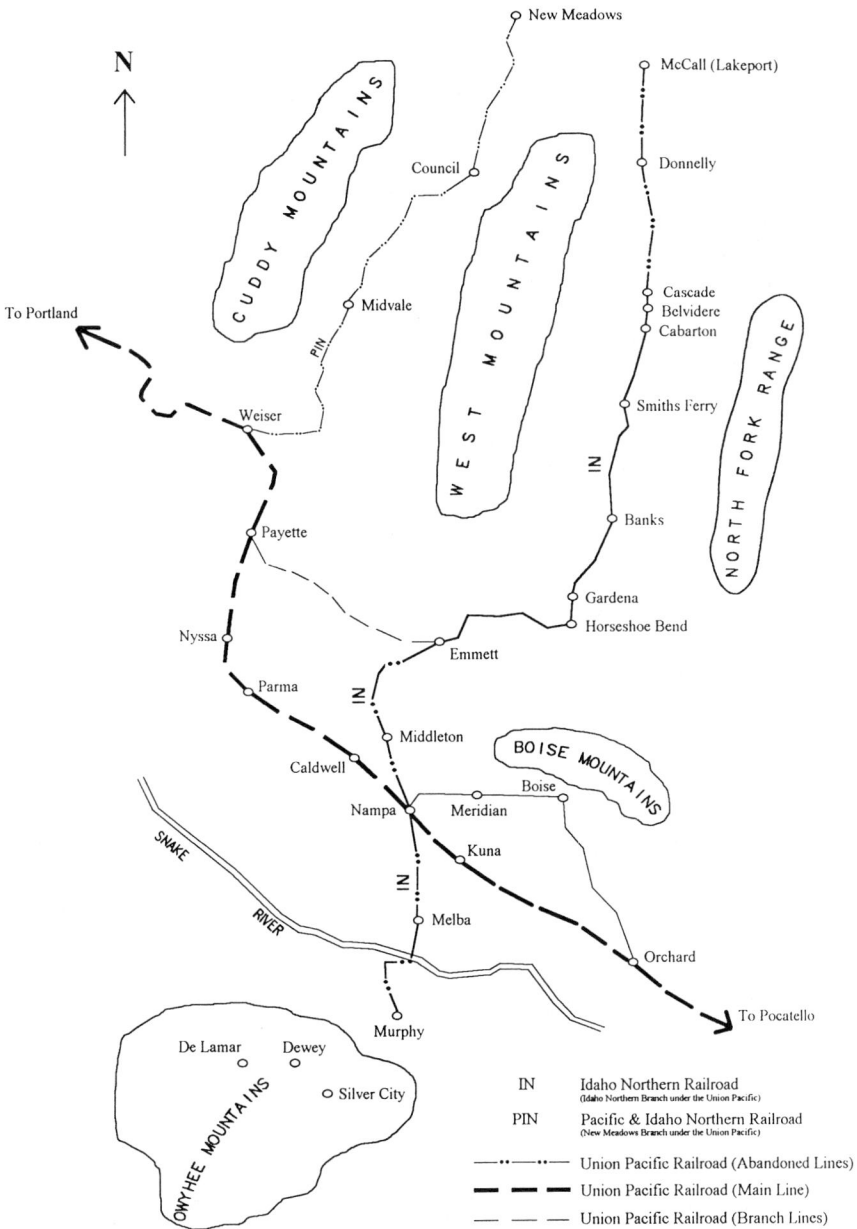

N

New Meadows

McCall (Lakeport)

CUDDY MOUNTAINS

Council

Donnelly

WEST MOUNTAINS

Midvale

Cascade
Belvidere
Cabarton

NORTH FORK RANGE

To Portland

PIN

Smiths Ferry

Weiser

IN

Payette

Banks

Nyssa

Gardena
Horseshoe Bend

Parma

Emmett

IN

Middleton

BOISE MOUNTAINS

Caldwell

Boise

Nampa

Meridian

SNAKE

Kuna

IN

RIVER

Melba

Orchard

To Pocatello

Murphy

De Lamar   Dewey

OWYHEE MOUNTAINS

Silver City

IN	Idaho Northern Railroad
	(Idaho Northern Branch under the Union Pacific)
PIN	Pacific & Idaho Northern Railroad
	(New Meadows Branch under the Union Pacific)

·—···—···—·· Union Pacific Railroad (Abandoned Lines)

▬ ▬ ▬ ▬ Union Pacific Railroad (Main Line)

— — — Union Pacific Railroad (Branch Lines)

2

Using the Guide

The Milepost Guide describes historic and scenic highlights along the railroad and is keyed to railroad mileposts near the track. The mileposts are numbered signs, visible from two directions, located on the east side of the railroad right-of-way. Numbers on the mileposts indicate the distance by rail from Nampa, where the Idaho Northern Railway started in the late 1890s.

Items of interest are listed in the Milepost Chapter of this book by the nearest milepost marker.

The Thunder Mountain Line operates the following regularly scheduled trains:
> ⇒ Cascade to Smiths Ferry - mileposts 99.7 to 82.71.
> ⇒ Horseshoe Bend to Banks - mileposts 49.64 to 63.88.

Introduction

Welcome aboard! Relax and enjoy as the Idaho Northern & Pacific Railroad takes you aboard the Thunder Mountain Line and transports you back to a time when folks moved at a slower pace and appreciated the simpler things in life.

The spectacular scenery along the line offers something for everyone, including sagebrush-covered hillsides, pristine forests, the narrow canyon shared with the Payette River, mountain meadows, and mountain farm and range lands. When nature cooperates, passengers can spot a variety of wildlife along the route, including fox, deer, elk, sandhill crane, blue heron, osprey, bald eagles and occasionally a moose or bear. During the summer months, passengers thrill at the sight of river rafters and kayakers as they challenge the powerful whitewater rapids of the Payette River.

"Whether you want scenery, mountain railroading, or just plain human interest, this line in western Idaho has them all," so said Trains Magazine in December 1947. The article was in reference to regular passenger service out of Valley County. This service was curtailed in 1949.

The Thunder Mountain Line had its inaugural run on July 4, 1998, and has been a popular attraction since. Passengers from all over the world enjoy a landscape that has changed very little since early pioneer days.

Our images of the Wild West and the frontier generally are formed by television and movies. They usually include covered wagons, cowboys, and Indians. Buffalo Bill, Wyatt Earp, Billy the Kid, and places like Tombstone, Arizona come readily to mind.

Rarely do we--those of us living in the West--realize that the Wild West and the frontier literally surround us. Less than one hundred years ago this place, right here, was the frontier. The history of Southwestern Idaho contains all the elements of a rousing novel, set in a land of vast and rugged beauty. Although time and progress have softened and tamed much of the West, there is still a wildness that remains.

Oregon Short Line depot at Nampa (about 1910), where the Idaho
Northern Railway originated. Photo courtesy of the Canyon County
Historical Society Museum.

Mileposts

26.93 Emmett
Elevation: 2373

1862 - Mountain man Tim Goodale guided the first
wagon train of sixty wagons down treacherous Freezout
Hill and across the Payette River where Emmett now
stands. The party consisted of emigrants headed for
Oregon and prospectors who were seeking a route to the
mines of Florence District in central Idaho.

At this time, gold was discovered in the Boise Basin and a
roadhouse was established east of Emmett, which was
known as Picket's Corral (spelling varies with different
sources; may also be spelled as Pickett). It soon became a

center of horse thieves and bogus gold-dust operators.
See: **Historical Vignettes, Picket's Corral**, page 66.

1861-1864 - Jonathan Smith and Nathaniel Martin settled
here and built a roadhouse, feed barn, post office, and
Martin's Ferry (also referred to as the Martindale Ferry or
Martinville Ferry by some). The roadhouse and ferry were
turned into a profitable venture by the traffic en route to
the Boise Basin mines. The growing settlement around
the ferry soon was called Martinsville.

1867 - Gold and silver were discovered at Pearl. By the
1890s, Pearl was a thriving community of 1,200 with the
typical mining town atmosphere of the time. Before the
boom fizzled in the early 1900s, several mines had
produced about $12 million in ore. Today, there is still an
operating mine at Pearl, but very little remains of the
original town.

Pearl was the first rest stop for stagecoaches bound from
Boise to the Squaw Creek Mining District and later to
Long Valley and Thunder Mountain.

1870 - Thomas Cahalan, a lawyer from Missouri,
established a post office west of Letha (seven miles west
of Martinsville) and named it Emmettville (or
Emmettsville) after his son Emmett. Six years later
Cahalan moved to Boise and the post office was relocated
to Martinsville, carrying its name with it.

1877 – Local legend says that a fort for protection from
the Indians was built near the present railroad depot
(probably at the outbreak of the Bannock War).

1883 - The current town was laid out with streets and lots
by James Wardel.

1900 - Emmettville incorporated and shortened its name to Emmett.

1902 - The Idaho Northern Railway reached Emmett in the spring. With railroad transportation, irrigation, good soil, and a moderate climate Emmett was set to become a boomtown. Over 26,000 acres were brought under irrigation and some 40,000 fruit trees were planted. By 1928, Emmett had become one of the largest shipping points on the Oregon Short Line (over 4,300 boxcar loads originated in Emmett in 1928 alone).

28.74 Last Chance Canal

31.71 Plaza

Not too far away, near the mouth of the canyon leading to Horseshoe Bend, is Picket's Corral, one of Idaho's most notorious outlaw hideouts during the 1860s. See: **Historical Vignettes, Picket's Corral**, page 66.

33.22 Black Canyon Dam

Black Canyon Dam is a concrete diversion dam that was constructed between 1922 and 1924, by the Bureau of Reclamation. A power plant was added in 1925 and contains two generators and two pump turbines. The construction camp for the dam was located at the site that is now occupied by Wild Rose Park. Four permanent five-room houses and 6 temporary cottages were built, along with a bathhouse, store, office building, mess hall, warehouse, and nine bunkhouses.

33.27 Tunnel No. 2
Length: 488 feet

The Oregon Short Line's Condensed Profile Index for the line shows this tunnel as the number two tunnel on the line and gives no indication of tunnel number one.

35.33 Johnson Creek

36.61 Anderson Creek

38.56 Tunnel No. 3
Length: 129 feet

39.44 Cherry Creek

41.01 Montour
Elevation: 2519

The most recent (1995) archaeological evidence dates human habitation of the Montour area 11,500 years ago, during the Winddust Period (a type of projectile point). Europeans came to the valley in the early 1860s, with discovery of gold in the Boise Basin, and used it as a range for their livestock. When the Idaho Northern reached the area in 1912, William Dewey, Jr. platted Montour, on the old Edson Marsh-John Ireton Ranch, which operated as a stage station for traffic headed to Placerville and Idaho City. Some think that Dewey's secretary suggested the name based on the French 'monture,' which means 'setting' or 'frame,' because of its pleasant environment. However, the newspapers of the time attribute the name to Mr. Montour an investor in the Dewey Syndicate. Montour quickly became the railroad shipping point for the rich Squaw Creek Valley and its principal towns of Sweet and Ola.

Completion of the Black Canyon Dam in 1924, destroyed the Payette River salmon run. Sediment gradually filled the reservoir, raising the water level and even flooding Montour. In 1973, remaining landowners and residents decided to sue the government, which began buying them out. Two years later the government razed the town's remaining buildings and Montour faded into history.

Montour depot, about 1915. H. A. Petersen Collection.

The old Montour area is now a designated wildlife sanctuary owned and maintained by the Bureau of Reclamation.

The dirt road that crosses the railroad tracks at Montour, at the site of the old depot, is the original stage road north from Boise, via Pearl.

Between Montour and the Black Canyon Reservoir was the site of the Squaw Creek Ferry. The Idaho Territorial Statesman reported on May 18, 1882:

> "Mitchell and Marsh have opened a ferry on the Payette River at Squaw Creek to aid travel to and from the Squaw Creek diggins (sic)."

42.45 Church Gulch

44.92 Rock Creek

49.08 Payette River

Next to the railroad bridge is the Boise Street Bridge, which was constructed in 1908, by J. H. Forbes of Caldwell for $4,680. According to the *Idaho Bridge Inventory*, this 184-foot bridge is the longest pony truss bridge of pin-connected type and the only Pratt half-hip truss bridge of more than one span in Idaho.

49.64 Horseshoe Bend
Elevation: 2614

Mahlon B. Moore, thought to be the first settler in the area, arrived with the Boise Basin gold rush in either 1862 or 1863. Initially settlers referred to the giant bend in the Payette river as 'The Big Bend' or 'The Bend.' The first name attached to the community that developed near the bend was 'Wardinerville,' named for Benjamin L. Wardiner, who built the first post office and became postmaster in October of 1865. On September 11, 1867, John A. Douglas, the new postmaster, changed the town's name to Horse Shoe Bend (original spelling).

During the gold rush, miners from the Boise Basin escaped the deep snows of the mountains and wintered in

The Bend. They also liked to leave their stock with the ranchers in the area while they headed up the old Harris Creek toll road to Placerville seeking their fortune. See: **Historical Vignettes, Picket's Corral**, page 66.

Frank R. Starr, city editor for the <u>San Francisco Chronicle</u>, visited the town of 300 in 1872, and reported:
> "The town is regularly laid out having a hotel, church, sawmill, schoolhouse, blacksmith shop, etc. The finest horses and cattle in the world are raised at Horse Shoe Bend and fattened on the luxurious hills. Extensive fishing is carried on here at certain times of the year."

Starr also reported seeing abundant sockeye and kokanee salmon in Payette Lake.

The railroad reached Horseshoe Bend in 1912, and constructed a two story depot in 1916, at the site where the Thunder Mountain Line depot is now located. The old railroad depot was saved from destruction and moved to its present location in 1986. It found a new life as 'The Old Riverside Depot Inn,' a bed & breakfast, situated on the north bank of the Payette River.

The town became quite a shipping center for the railroad for livestock as well as logs. Large corrals were built between what is now the medical clinic and the old Boise Cascade mill property. In the fall, sheep would be herded through town and were held in the corrals until they could be shipped out via the railroad. Cattle were shipped regularly to Denver, Portland, Omaha, and Chicago.

The original town of Horse Shoe Bend existed on the south side of the Payette River. With the arrival of the Idaho Northern, the 'new' Horseshoe Bend was created as a town company by the railroad on the north bank of the river. A town company was formed by the railroad to buy large tracks of land and sell lots, similar to real estate developers of today.

Several coal mines where located in the Horseshoe Bend area. One of the largest was the Hi Henry Mine, which was located on Cottonwood Creek Road, south of town.

The old railroad coach that is located near the Thunder Mountain Line depot is an old Northern Pacific Coach. The car, which was numbered 1031, was one of a group of fifty, 70-foot, First Class coaches bought from Barney & Smith of Dayton, Ohio, in 1907 (the series was numbered 1000 through 1049). The cars were straight truss rod, wood construction, with arched stained-glass windows and teak panel interiors. Car 1031 saw service on the Northern Pacific's Yellowstone Park Route until about 1928, and was retired at the railroad's South Tacoma (Washington) Shops in August of 1942. It is thought that in July of 1923, the car carried part of President Warren G. Harding's party as he traveled to Yellowstone. In September 1944, it was returned to service as Outfit Car No X-130. At some later date it was again retired from service and the body was sold. Between 1960 and 1985, the car had various owners. It was purchased in 1985, by the owners of a Givens Hot Springs, resort near Murphy, Idaho. They moved it from Washington State, with the intention of converting it into a restaurant. The restaurant plans did not materialize and the car sat in the Idaho desert for nearly 15 years. Over the years, its stained glass windows served as targets for rocks and its teak interior as fuel for campfires.

The coach was moved in November of 1999, by the Scenic Payette River Historical Society, to Horseshoe Bend for restoration.

52.39 Hell Roaring Gulch

53.0 Porter Creek

53.73 Calamity Gulch

53.8 Climax Rapids
Class III rapids (Milepost location is approximate.)

54.5 Hill Creek

54.87 Gardena
Elevation: 2684

It is thought that Gardena received its name in 1914, from officials of the Oregon Short Line in an apparent attempt to make the area attractive to prospective settlers.

A history of Gardena as gleaned from the book "Examining our Roots, a History of the Horseshoe Bend Area," by Maryjane Dobson and Margarete Drake, published August 1990, provided by C. L. Wolfkiel:
"E. B. Darnielle and his wife had a store with warehouses for coal, stock salt, grain, and sundry articles of freight near railroad milepost 54. This facility, which included a post office until 1954, was located on the west side of the tracks initially and sometime after the Gardena bridge was built in 1920, was moved to the east side where the current Highway 55 was constructed in 1924. Sometime after the Gardena Store was moved to the east side of the river, it was owned by Sam and

13

Elizabeth (Lib) Raft Charters. "Sam & Lib's" was a familiar stopping place to those who frequented the north-south highway. Sam was a Boise County Deputy Sheriff for 21 years, and it was laughingly said that it was the only place in Idaho where you could drink a beer while taking your driver's test.

"Gardena at various times was a significant shipping point on the railroad for logs, beef cattle, sheep and wool. North, above Gardena, was the Sherard Mine, and there were others in the Jerusalem area with names unknown. Deposits of coal have also been found in Jerusalem Valley. Some ore may have also been shipped from here.

"Prior to the construction of the Gardena bridge, fording the river or using a cable car, were the two ways of getting between the east and west banks. The 1910, Payette Lakes Wagon Road and the Oregon Shortline Railroad, built in 1912, were both located on the west side of the river. On the east side there was the significant population in Jerusalem Valley needing access to the road and railroad prior to the construction of Highway 55.

"Jerusalem is an area with no known boundaries due east from Gardena, whose history is very intertwined with that of Horseshoe Bend and Gardena. In the 1860s, several families homesteaded in the Jerusalem Valley and established the first permanent agriculture in the area, predating that in the Boise Valley.

"The Brownlee Trail, which crossed the Payette River just north of Gardena, was the most important trail for those coming from the west, providing passage for early explorers, trappers, and miners. The trail began in Oregon, crossing the Snake River just above Hell's Canyon and then on to the Weiser River. From there it followed Crane Creek, over a pass to Squaw Creek about fifteen miles above the present town of Ola. It then crossed Little Squaw Creek, followed Soldier Creek over Timber Butte to Brownlee Creek, and finally down the ford on the Payetter River, at Frenchmen's Island. Before the appearance of the Europeans, the trail was used by the Umatilla Indians going to and from their annual tribal council in the Council Valley on the Weiser River near the current town of Council."

The Gardena Bridge connects present-day Gardena to Highway 55 and was erected in 1920, by the Missouri Valley Bridge and Iron Company of Leavenworth, Kansas. This structure is the longest multiple span pony truss bridge in Idaho and is the only such structure built by the contractor in the state.

55.20 Brownlee Creek

55.5 Frenchman's Island
The island, located approximately one mile north of Gardena, was named for Jean and Pierre Mouferon, two Frenchmen who for years raised produce here, including watermelons.

On June 2, 1863, Phillip Remmil obtained a license to operate the first ferry on the Payette on the northern part of the island. The ferry served prospectors who came to the area via the Brownlee Trail during the Boise Basin gold rush.

56.7 Cottonwood Creek
(Milepost location is approximate.)

56.8 AMF Rapids
Class III rapids (Milepost location is approximate.)

AMF is an acronym that stands for 'Adios Mother F----r.' Running the length of the Payette takes skill and courage and early river pioneers were so elated when they had survived the run that they named these last major rapids accordingly.

57.05 Mixmaster Rapids
Class III rapids (Milepost location is approximate.)

57.06 Boulder Creek

58.4 Mike's Hole Rapids
Class III rapids (Milepost location is approximate.)

58.7 Fleming Creek
(Milepost location is approximate.)

61.7 Bennett's Rock Rapids
Class II rapids (Milepost location is approximate.)

Bennett's Rock (also called Bennett's Hole by some) is named because of the large boulder in the middle of the river. The name Bennett came from a man who used to run a restaurant in what was the lower portion of Banks. The buildings in this part of Banks were destroyed in a mudslide in 1996.

62.0 Lunch Counter Rapids
Class II rapids (Milepost location is approximate.)

Named "Lunch Counter" because kayakers and rafters like to eat lunch on the right bank and watch the action on the river.

62.53 Dry Buck Creek

63.1 Surf City Rapids
Class II rapids (Milepost location is approximate.)

63.5 Second Bend Rapids
Class II rapids (Milepost location is approximate.)

63.87 Whitewater 101 Rapids
Class II rapids (Milepost location is approximate.)

63.88 Banks
Elevation: 2809

Banks is a small village named for the Banks family. W. B. Banks was a local rancher and Emma Banks the first postmaster.

The Idaho Northern constructed a two-story depot, section house, crew quarters, two-stall engine house, coal shed, water tower, and an arm-strong turntable at Banks. Helper engines were stationed here with their crews to assist northbound trains over the 2.8% grade between Banks and Smiths Ferry.

During the days of passenger travel on the railroad, a hotel and restaurant offered travelers an opportunity to get some rest and have a meal.

Diesel power eliminated the need for helpers along the line and most structures, with the exception of the section house, were razed over the years. While diesel locomotives eliminated the need for helper engines, the actual time required for a train to travel from Emmett to Cascade has changed very little over the past 90 years. Just as they did in 1914, the trains of today still travel no faster than 10-25 miles per hour along the line. Banks is still the meeting and interchange point between northbound trains coming from Emmett and southbound trains from Cascade.

UP 605, 2-8-0 switching at Banks in 1941. H. A. Petersen Collection. H. R. Griffiths photo.

The Rivers and Rails lower run is a family adventure that combines a historic railroad excursion with the excitement of river rafting. This combined package is presented by the Thunder Mountain Line and the Cascade Raft & Kayak Company on the Main Payette between Horseshoe Bend and Banks. The three-hour splashy getaway is perfect for everyone--especially families, first-timers, groups, and tours.

64.7 Crunch Rapids
Class V rapids (Milepost location is approximate.)

65.06 Phillips Creek

68.3 Hound's Tooth Rapids
Class V rapids (Milepost location is approximate.)

Named after the 'two big teeth' sticking up at the beginning of the rapids.

65.8 Juicer Rapids
Class V rapids (Milepost location is approximate.)

66.7 Otter's Run Rapids
Class V rapids (Milepost location is approximate.)

Named after the otters that can frequently be spotted here.

66.83 Payette River
The 484-foot bridge consists of two Warren truss deck spans over the river and four steel girder approach spans and is the only Warren truss deck railroad bridge in the state.

The bridge was also a favorite photo spot for W. H. Griffiths, Jr. a noted railroad photographer.

69.2 Jaws I, II, III Rapids
Class V rapids (Milepost location is approximate.)

70.1 Screaming Left/Island Rapids
Class V rapids (Milepost location is approximate.)

Train 385 with engines 254, 735 and 757 approaching milepost 66.83 on September 1, 1947. H. A. Petersen Collection. H. R. Griffiths photo.

70.7 Howell Creek
(Milepost location is approximate.)

71.0 Williams Creek
(Milepost location is approximate.)

71.1 Golf Course Rapids
Class V rapids (Milepost location is approximate.)

An almost endless series of holes (more than 18) and rocks for a little over a mile.

72.3 Jacob's Ladder Rapids
Class V rapids (Milepost location is approximate.)

Jacob's Ladder drops nearly 265 feet in less than a mile.

72.9 Pectoralis Major Rapids
Class V rapids (Milepost location is approximate.)

73.9 Bouncer Down the Middle Rapids
Class V rapids (Milepost location is approximate.)

74.4 Chaos Rapids
Class V rapids (Milepost location is approximate.)

74.6 Nowhere to Run Rapids
Class V rapids (Milepost location is approximate.)

Nowhere to Run deserves its name because there is no safe and simple way to get through it.

74.8 Bad Jose Rapids
Class V rapids (Milepost location is approximate.)

75.0 Slide Rapids
Class V rapids (Milepost location is approximate.)

The cable footbridge that spans the river marks the beginning of this rapid. The rapid is a steep drop with no distinguishing characteristics and was named because it looks and feels like a slide when paddling though it.

75.36 Big Eddy
Elevation: 4089

Big Eddy was the site of a big splash dam during the days the river was used for floating logs down to Emmett. With the arrival of the railroad a siding, water tower, and a coal shed were built here as well.

75.7 S-turn Rapids
Class V rapids (Milepost location is approximate.)

Named for several s-turns the river makes at this location.

77.34 Tunnel No. 4
Length: 221 feet

78.5 Disneyland Rapids
Class V rapids (Milepost location is approximate.)

Named by John Wasson after the ultimate E-ticket ride in Disneyland.

78.6 Rat Creek

79.0 Nutcracker Rapids
Class V rapids (Milepost location is approximate.)

Nutcracker is considered one of the toughest drops on the Payette. According to Stephen Stuebner and his book Paddling the Payette, "John Wasson, who ran most of the North Fork with a group of five expert kayakers in 1979, says they named this drop as such because it is shaped like a nutcracker, with the hole or rock serving as the 'nut,' but the rapid has a nice double-meaning, too. If you fail to avoid the 'nut' feature, you're likely to get squeezed as if you're between the clamps of a nutcracker."

79.5 Steepness Rapids
Class V rapids (Milepost location is approximate.)

Named because of the steep five-foot shelf that the river drops over. This 15-mile section of the North Fork of the Payette, between Smiths Ferry and Banks, is considered one of the most challenging Class V whitewater runs in North America.

82.71 Smiths Ferry
Elevation: 4538

1883 – Site of a Coe & Carter logging camp. See also: **Loggers and River Hogs**, page 37.

1884 – James Smith established a ferryboat at the present site of Cougar Mountain Lodge. Actually Smith bought the ferry from Clinton Meyers and it was Smith's name rather than Meyers' name that stuck to the place. To compound confusion, the post office and way station at Smiths Ferry were actually named Fern. Upon its arrival the railroad named its station Smiths Ferry, which eventually was adopted by the post office and the community as a whole.

1898 – Peter Neebs established the post office at 'Fern' near the present site of Smiths Ferry.

1913 - The first train into Smiths Ferry arrived in early August and is described as follows by Gratia Bacon Matthews:

"In August 1913, the Railroad Company decided to have an excursion over the new road from Nampa to Smiths Ferry. They brought three coaches loaded with sightseers… That special August day in 1913, a large crowd had gathered. Wagons, buggies, and saddle horses where lined up along the road toward the river. Teams had been unhitched and horses tied to the wheels of the vehicles, where they were eating from hay in the wagon or from grain in nosebags.

"Everyone waited with great expectations, for something of importance was about to happen. History was being made. Our lives would never be the same again, but we didn't know it then.

"At last we heard a mighty whistle. Then the train choo-chooing along came in view, and on up the meadow, stopping at the road where it was greeted by the cheers of the waiting people.

"Mr. Lou Gorton and his wife, Maggie, had the Smiths Ferry hotel at the time. Maggie was a lively person. As the engine stopped steaming and groaning, she pretended to go wild with fright. Some cowboys lassoed her and tied her to a fence."

1930 - The Smiths Ferry Civilian Conservation Corps camp began in 1930, under the presidency of Herbert Hoover during the Great Depression. The men that lived in this camp constructed Rainbow Bridge, Highway 55, the lookout on East Mountain, and several other forest projects. Sometime in the 1940s, the camp was sold to Boise Payette Lumber and eventually passed to the Southern Idaho Timber Association. Today, the camp is the Payette River Lodge and is undergoing extensive renovation.

Train 386, with engine 611, a 2-8-0, at Smiths Ferry on November 20, 1941. H. A. Petersen Collection. H. R. Griffiths photo.

83.5 Howard's Plunge Rapids
Class III rapids (Milepost location is approximate.)

Allegedly named after a guy who drove off the road and into the river, not once, but twice!

83.72 Tunnel No. 5
Tunnel No 5 with a length of 37 feet has the distinction of being the shortest solid-rock rock railroad tunnel in North America. Make sure you don't blink your eyes or you will have missed it.

83.7 Little Bogus Creek

84.6 Francois Rapids
Class III rapids (Milepost location is approximate.)

Named after Francois Payette.

The shortest solid-rock railroad tunnel in North America, ca. 1915. Note the absence of Highway 55 on the left side of the river. H. A. Petersen Collection.

84.8 Smoothie Rapids
Class II-III rapids (Milepost location is approximate.)

85.12 Rainbow Bridge
Elevation: 4494

Listed on the National Register of Historic Places, Rainbow Bridge was constructed in 1933, by C. F. Dinsmore & Co. of Ogden, Utah. To this day, the 410-foot-long bridge remains the largest single-span concrete arch in Idaho. It has been an icon for generations of Idaho travelers, so much so that its image is the official logo for the highway's designation as the Payette River Scenic Byway. A note of interest: In 1998, a couple exchanged marriage vows on the train under the bridge.

In 1934, the Idaho Statesman wrote what still is true today:
> "Only too often the works of men in the wilderness are a blot on the landscape. Roads make great ugly scars through the forest; bridges are stark, graceless structures of red-painted steelwork. And with this in mind, many people were privately concerned when it was announced the state would build a bridge across the Payette River in the beautiful canyon above Smiths Ferry.

> "But they were needlessly concerned. The bridge now completed and ready for use is one of the most beautiful structures of any kind in the state."

Present-day Highway 55 from Smiths Ferry to Round Valley actually follows the old railroad construction road. The old road from Smiths Ferry to Round Valley was via Neebs Hill, which runs east of Smiths Ferry.

85.25 Round Valley Creek
Round Valley Creek, originally called Railroad Creek by railroad construction crews who had a construction camp nearby.

86.1 Wet Spot Rapids
Class III rapids (Milepost location is approximate.)

The area was the location of a railroad construction camp in 1912.

87.8 Boulder Creek

89.5 Fawn Creek

89.5-89.9 Trestle Rapids
Class III rapids (Milepost location is approximate.)

89.59 Steel Trestle
Elevation: 4730
The steel girder-bridge over Trestle Rapids was constructed in 1913.

89.6 Rafting
The Rivers and Rails upper run is a cooperative effort between the Thunder Mountain Line and Idaho Whitewater Unlimited. This unique trip combines the nostalgia and excitement of a historic rail trip with the thrills of whitewater rafting. Passengers ride the Thunder Mountain Line from Smiths Ferry to this location, where they are off-loaded, along with rafts and related river gear, to float back downstream.

91.6 Hurdy Creek

91.9 Old Siding

Between 1912-1913, the site was the location of a railroad construction camp. From 1920-1923, the siding was used as a logging siding by Art "Donkey" Campbell, a private contractor for the Boise Payette Lumber, who specialized in high-lead (donkey) logging. Since there was no other road into the area, this was also referred to as a walk-in camp.

92.66 Cabarton
Elevation: 4654

Cabarton was named for Charles A. Barton, the General Manager of the Boise Payette Lumber Company.

In 1902, a Weyerhaeuser syndicate formed the Payette Lumber and Manufacturing Company at Emmett, with the intent to log along the Payette and float the logs down the river to Emmett. Floating the Payette required extensive channeling of the river and a huge splash dam at Big Eddy. In the long run, floating did not work and the lumber company had to wait for the railroad to arrive.

In 1913, Payette Lumber was merged with Barber Lumber; another Weyerhaeuser held company, to create Boise Payette Lumber. Most of the new company's executives and a large part of the workforce that came to Long Valley were from Northland Pine in Minnesota, a Weyerhaeuser operation that was closing down. Charles A. Barton who was General Manager at Northland became General Manager at Boise Payette.

Logging began in 1916, in Crawford Nook and on Cascade Ridge. In an effort to avoid taxes, headquarters of the operation were established outside Cascade city limits at what is now the Waters Edge RV Park. Eager to enlarge its revenue base, Cascade battled Boise Payette for two years in an attempt to annex the area. When Cascade finally extended its city limits, Boise Payette responded by moving its headquarters, buildings and all, to a new location, calling it Cabarton.

To complete the move, the company needed to construct the amenities that Cascade had provided--a school, a store, and a single men's boarding house. These, along with the locomotive shed were the only permanent structures; all other buildings were temporary and 'portable.' Cabarton, which never incorporated, was awarded post office status on March 15, 1919, listing Edgar MacGregor--Northland's former Woods Boss (chief of logging operations)--as postmaster and town manager. Cabarton existed until 1935, as half town and half logging camp. In 1935, the town was put on flatcars and relocated to the Gold Fork (between Cascade and McCall) and became the town of MacGregor.

95.32 Belvidere
Elevation: 4747

Mr. Belvidere was another friend of the Dewey family who was to have his name bestowed upon a thriving community. However, the community of Belvidere never amounted to much, never becoming more than a water stop, complete with water tower, for the railroad. The few references that exist to Mr. Belvidere indicate that at times he was a spokesman for the syndicate during the railroad's construction.

97.0 – Logging Railroads

Old logging railroad grades branch off to the west towards what Boise Payette called Cascade Ridge. See also: **Logging Railroads**, page 57.

99.11 - Cascade

Elevation: 4746
Population: 1001

Most towns in Long Valley grew up around a post office, but Cascade had its start with a railroad depot. As the Oregon Short Line was constructing its line through the valley in 1913, it bypassed the towns of Van Wyck, Crawford, and Thunder City. The railroad located its depot near the falls on the Payette River and called it Cascade.

Bypassing the existing towns was done intentionally in order for the railroad to get land at cheaper prices, develop its own town-sites, and to profit from the resulting land sales. Mr. Belvidere, like Montour and Donnelly, were investors with Dewey and were to have their names bestowed upon thriving communities. Even though the Dewey Syndicate no longer owned the Idaho Northern by the time it was completed, it still owned thousands of acres of land along the surveyed right-of-way. This ownership still influenced the Oregon Short Line's construction of the line. Thus began the continuing and never settled argument about whether the railroad deliberately bypassed the existing towns to enhance the syndicate rather than following the most direct route.

The town site of Cascade was platted in 1913, and became the county seat in 1917. Cascade supplanted the nearby towns of Van Wyck, Crawford and Thunder City, while Donnelly made the town of Roseberry obsolete.

Locations:

- The falls for which Cascade was named were located at the site of the dam north of town.
- Crawford was located at the end of the falls, near the highway bridge.
- Van Wyck is now under Lake Cascade.
- Thunder City was located east of Cascade on Gold Dust Road.
- Headquarters for the Boise Payette Lumber Company was located at the present-day site of the Waters Edge RV Park.
- The Cascade railroad depot is now located on the western side of the Cascade Airport at the southern end of town.
- The remains of an old trestle from a logging railroad can be seen crossing the river near the Highway 55 overpass at the north end of town when the water level is low.

See also: **Colonel W. H. Dewey**, page 40, **Thunder Mountain**, page 43, and **History of the Idaho Northern**, page 47.

99.7 - End of the line
Today, the railroad abruptly ends at the north end of Cascade. The segment from Cascade to McCall was abandoned by the Union Pacific Railroad on May 14, 1980.

The rail embankment was built before Highway 55 came through town in order to gain altitude to climb over the hill to the north. The rail segment just below the embankment to the east is a remnant of the spur that went into the old Boise Payette Lumber Headquarters.

Geology

Most of the Payette River Basin cuts through a large homogenous granite rock formation known as the Idaho Batholith. This formation underlies most of Central Idaho and was formed as a giant magma bubble 50 to 70 million years ago. As this bubble slowly rose and compressed, it produced one of the largest bodies of granite in the world. The southern portion of the batholith, the part dominating most of the Payette River Basin, is called the Atlanta Lobe.

The numerous hot springs in the region are evidence of the many fault lines that are beneath the surface. They occasionally rattle the area with earthquakes.

Early Inhabitants

Archaeological evidence shows that human occupation of the region dates back at least 11,500 years. The Native Americans lived peacefully off the rich bounty of plants, berries, fish and wildlife. This group of the Northern Shoshoni, called "Tukudeka" (Tookoo-dee-ka) chose to live in isolation in the grassy meadows and high mountain valleys of the Salmon River country. Mountain sheep constituted a large part of their diet, and "Tukudeka" literally means "eaters of white meat/animals." Early explorers and trappers referred to these native people as "Sheepeaters".

The Indians in the region led a relatively peaceful life until the 1860s, when large numbers of European and Chinese moved into the Boise Basin in search of gold. The Indians avoided the ever-increasing number of homesteads and settlements in the area and retreated into the backcountry.

The Trappers

The Payette River was named by Francois Payette, a very colorful French Canadian trapper and mountain man. Payette, whose date of birth is unknown, was originally from Saint Roch de L'Assomption, a small town near Montreal. In 1810, he went to work for John Jacob Astor's Pacific Fur Company and was among the party that build Fort Astoria at the mouth of the Columbia River. In 1814, he transferred to the Northwest Company when Astor sold his business to the Canadian firm.

Payette first set eyes on the Payette River, which he immediately named for himself, in 1817, as a member of the first "Snake River Expedition," under the leadership of Donald McKenzie. For the next four years McKenzie and his men worked an area that stretched from the Grand Tetons in the east, the Great Salt Lake in the south, the Cascades to the west, and the Salmon River canyon to the north.

Payette was a character who inspired novels and movies. He was a skilled hunter and trapper, fought bloody battles with the Indians, and managed to survive in hostile territory long after others had left. Later in life, the Hudson Bay Company made him master of Fort Boise, where he 'wined and dined' Oregon Trail emigrants with fresh dairy products, salmon, sturgeon, and other delicacies. In 1843, Payette retired from the Hudson Bay Company and returned to Montreal. It is unclear where and when he died and where he was buried. Some believe that he died in a French-Canadian village, while others

think he died in Payette, Idaho, and was buried
overlooking the Snake River.

The Miners

The event that brought the most abrupt change to the
Indians' way of life was the discovery of gold in central
Idaho in 1860. Gold strikes in the Grimes Creek area of
the Boise Basin in 1862, brought thousands of miners to
the area. Although the big strikes were over the mountains
to the south of Long Valley, prospectors traveled through
the Payette River country to get there. Some paused long
enough to pan the creeks of the valley, but the deposits
found were not extensive. The few claims that existed in
Long Valley were only worked in the summer.

The typical route from the West was the Brownlee Trail,
which crossed the Payette River near the present-day
town of Gardena. Prospectors arriving from the north
came into the basin via Alder Creek and Grimes Pass.

Trouble in the Valley

Ranchers from the Boise Valley to the south and the
Indian Valley to the west often drove their stock to
summer ranges in the valley.

In August of 1878, trouble erupted between some
renegade Indians and a handful of whites near Cascade.
On August 17, 1878, Indian Valley pioneer William
Monday discovered that some of his mares had been
stolen. Monday saw moccasin tracks on the trail and
determined to get his horses back. Against the advice of
everyone he knew, he gathered up three friends, Sylvester

35

"Three-fingered" Smith, Tom Healy and Jake Grosclose, and followed the trail into Long Valley.

The men, heavily armed, crossed the Payette River at the "Narrows", north of present-day Cascade, and headed north into an Indian ambush. Monday, who was in the lead, was killed instantly with three bullets in the heart. The others scrambled for cover, without much success. Grosclose and Healy quickly met the same fate as Monday. Smith was shot through the hip and arm, but managed to retreat on his mule by reversing direction. During his flight, he fell off his mule, tumbled down the mountain slope, and hid inside a beaver lodge on the edge of the river. Smith hid in the lodge until after dark and swam to an island where he hid for two days.

On the third night he hiked toward Payette Lake, 25 miles away, and intercepted the mail carrier. Smith was taken to New Meadows and a man was dispatched to Boise to summon medical help.

A contingent of the U.S. Cavalry, under the leadership of a major named Drum, camped near the headwaters of the Weiser River 13 miles from New Meadows, was quickly alerted. Major Drum immediately pursued the Indians and discovered two more dead bodies eight miles east of where Monday and his two friends were killed. The troops continued the pursuit for several more days, until they were forced to return for more supplies.

These events, combined with the prior murder of five Chinese miners on Loon Creek and an attack on other settlers near Warren, led to an all-out assault on the Indians in Central Idaho. General Oliver O. Howard sent three troops of soldiers and scouts into the region to apprehend the Indians. The Indians, who knew the area better than the soldiers, started brush and forest fires to push the cavalry back, then hid in the canyons and mountain meadows that they knew so well.

By October 1, 1879, one of the troops had captured about 50 Indians, who where taken to Fort Vancouver and delivered to General Howard. The following year they were moved to the Fort Hall Indian Reservation north of Pocatello.

The Sheepeater War was the only major skirmish between the Indians and the whites in the Payette Basin. A peaceful band of the Sheepeaters lived in the Dry Buck area above Banks and Squaw Creek Valley until the late 1800s.

Loggers and River Hogs

It was the construction of the Oregon Short Line Railroad (OSL) through Idaho that in the early 1880s was ultimately responsible for increased homesteading and the creation of permanent settlements in Long Valley--30 years before its actual arrival in the valley itself.

As the OSL was constructing its line through southern Idaho in 1882-1884, a shortage of railroad ties created the need for the first Payette River log drive. In 1883, logging contractor Coe & Carter, of Omaha, Nebraska, brought woodsmen from Maine and the Midwest to cut logs for railroad ties in the North Fork drainage of the Payette River. The company had been awarded the contract to supply the railroad with 300,000 railroad ties. Over 300 men came to the area and set up two camps, one at Smiths Ferry and the other at Tamarack Swamp in Long Valley. Logs were cut and shaped into ties and then floated down

the river to Boomerang. The town was on the opposite
site of the river from present day Payette (its name has
nothing to do with Australia and was based on the hero in
a series of dime novels).

Train 385 with engines 526, 529 and 757 (all 2-8-0) near Big Eddy on
July 28, 1948. H. A. Petersen Collection. H. R. Griffiths photo.

Log drives on the Payette were daring and very
dangerous, for loggers not only floated the logs and
railroad ties down river, but also followed them in
wooden boats. Loggers and rivermen (a.k.a. "River
Hogs"), who had no life jackets, drowned nearly every
year.

Towns Established

As the loggers worked in the area, the beauty and
abundance of resources captivated them. Some planned
on returning and wrote to their friends and families to
come and join them.

The original homesteads were constructed of hand-hewn logs, with dirt or puncheon floors. Puncheon floors consisted of logs split in half and laid with the flat side up. Mud or clay was used for chinking between the logs. Ceilings, doors, casings, furniture, as well as the shingles on the roof were made of boards split by hand.

In those days, people were largely self-sufficient and literally lived off the land. Animal skins were tanned for gloves, leggings, shoes, and even hinges. Grass and wild hay were cut by hand and bundled into shocks to stand on end in the field to dry. In late summer or early fall, it was gathered on wagons and stored in barns or haystacks.

As more people discovered the valley and began to homestead, towns like Van Wyck, Arling, and Crawford developed. Thunder City (town site is east of Cascade on Gold Dust Road) had its beginnings in the late 1890s as the discovery of gold on Thunder Mountain (near Yellow Pine) spurred yet another gold rush. The town was established as the supply center for the remote mines.

Colonel W. H. Dewey, about 1900. Photo courtesy of the Canyon
County Historical Society Museum.

Colonel W. H. Dewey

Colonel William H. Dewey never was a Colonel. The
Owyhee Avalanche newspaper invented the title. Born
August 1, 1823, in Adams, Massachusetts, the young
Dewey ran away from home at age eleven and made his
way to Buffalo, New York where he found a job driving
mules on the Erie Canal. By the time he was fifteen, he
owned two barges of his own. At the age of twenty he had
a $20,000 fortune, had built the first penny arcade in the
United States, and owned a sawmill, a shingle mill, and a
livery stable. If that was not enough, there is speculation
that he also smuggled horses from Canada by swimming
them across the Niagara River at night.

When he was nearly forty, he went to San Francisco
where he and a man named Michael Jordan started a
contracting business that did not last long. Dewey and his
partner were soon drawn by the "gold fever" to Virginia
City, Nevada, where they struck out and lost most of their
fortune.

Hearing of the riches to be found in Idaho, Dewey and
Jordan decided to seek their fortunes there. Dewey, who
had contracted malaria when he sailed to San Francisco
via Panama, stayed in Virginia City, while Jordan went
ahead. On August 27, 1863, Dewey finally set out on foot
to make the 400-mile journey from Virginia City to the
Owyhee Mountains in Idaho, where he arrived on
November 24, 1863. Within seven days, Dewey had
struck it rich but also lost his partner Michael Jordan, who
was killed by hostile Indians. By 1870, Dewey was 47
years old and owned half of the successful South
Mountain Camp.

Dewey not only was a risk taker, builder, organizer, promoter, and speculator, but also was a show-off, and spent money lavishly, to the point that he was reckless.

In 1884, at age 61, Dewey was involved in a shoot-out with a bartender in Silver City. On October 2, 1884, Dewey was convicted of manslaughter and sentenced to eight years at hard labor in the territorial prison at Boise. He subsequently appealed his sentence and was acquitted in May of 1885, of all charges on grounds of self-defense. Dewey's legal expenses and the collapse of the Bank of California however, had left him $40,000 in debt and without credit.

Dewey was not down and out for long. By 1886, following the discovery of a rich gold vein in Florida Mountain near Silver City, he was back in business. He purchased and developed the Trade Dollar Mine, which he later sold for over one (or eleven) million dollars-- records give conflicting information on the amount. He engaged in road building in Owyhee County and established the town of Dewey, three miles from Silver City, in 1896.

At century's end, Dewey was the head of the Dewey Syndicate, which included investors from Pittsburgh, Pennsylvania, and Longfellow Oil of Ohio, and his local empire spread from the Payette headwaters to the Owyhee mining district, south of Murphy. To serve the mines, Dewey built the Boise, Nampa & Owyhee Railroad to Murphy in 1897, and for his Payette River interests, which included the mining districts at Buffalo Hump and Thunder Mountain, he incorporated the Idaho Northern Railway on December 14, 1897.

Thunder Mountain

Thunder Mountain is located in the Frank Church Wilderness, about 30 miles northeast of Yellow Pine. Today, it has the little known distinction as the site of the last gold rush in the United States. Its epicenter is on the town of Roosevelt, which is now at the bottom of Roosevelt Lake.

The Thunder Mountain Mining district was on Monumental Creek, which drains into Big Creek, which in turn empties into the Salmon River. Ultimately, it was the Sheepeater War in 1879, which opened the area for prospecting. In its effort to suppress the Indians, the US Army built a military road through the area. With the road in place and the Indian threat neutralized, mining began on Big Creek in 1883. By 1885, a new mining district, named the Alton District, had been formed further west. Prospectors from Alton found good ore on Monumental Creek in 1890, and in 1896, the Caswell Brothers patented 14 claims on Mule Creek, a tributary of Monumental. It was on these Caswell claims that the Thunder Mountain District would begin. Thunder Mountain eventually would absorb the Alton and Big Creek districts and would become so vast, that in 1905, it would unsuccessfully apply to the Idaho Legislature to become Mineral County.

There were initially only two roads--packhorse trails, which were considered roads at the time--into this huge district. The oldest, based on the military road, came east from Warren, over Elk Creek Summit. The second, named Boise Road, was begun in 1890, and ran from Boise to Idaho City, Banner Summit, Bear Valley and Pen Basin (Deadwood). Neither of these roads could handle sufficient freight for the district to evolve into a major producer.

In 1897/1898, Colonel W. H. Dewey and his Dewey Syndicate, who knew of the suspected wealth of the region, became involved in prospecting Thunder Mountain and Buffalo Hump further north.

The Dewey Syndicate formed the Idaho Northern Railway as a subsidiary of the Boise, Nampa & Owyhee, which was being built from Nampa to Silver City, with the ultimate objective of Winnemucca, Nevada. The Idaho Northern was to run from Nampa to Butte, Montana, via the Salmon River, thus serving both Buffalo Hump and Thunder Mountain. The Idaho Northern bonds were bought by the Oregon Short Line, for no other reason than to keep them from falling into the hands of the Northern Pacific.

In 1899, the syndicate, as Dewey Consolidated Mining & Smelting, bought the five best claims at Buffalo Hump and in 1900, began buying the Caswell Brothers' 14 claims on Mule Creek at Thunder Mountain.

The media dutifully reported these developments and began touting Thunder Mountain as the next American gold rush. The two preceding mining media events at Cripple Creek, Colorado, and the Klondyke, were fading news. Media claims that 30 pounds of gold could be had for 42 hours work at Thunder Mountain helped to set the stage, and when Dewey gave the Caswells a check for $100,000 for their claims on November 15, 1901, the rush was on.

What the prospectors did not know was that the Dewey Syndicate and rival investors already held all the good

44

properties by the summer of 1901. The much-publicized November payment amounted to nothing more than a promotional stunt.

Nevertheless, 175 additional claims were added by the rushers (prospectors) over the winter, before the main body of prospectors arrived in 1902. Of these, 17 were staked in the snow without even prospecting, and 16 of these actually turned out to be good paying claims.

By the summer of 1902, there were an estimated 7,000 prospectors in the district. The town and post office of Roosevelt, named for President Teddy Roosevelt, were formed that summer. Roosevelt was a company town that was owned by the Dewey Syndicate. But with the best claims already held by the syndicates, the population in the district had dwindled to 350 by 1903. The Thunder Mountain Gold Rush, the last in the United States, had lasted less than one year.

Disaffected rushers would go into other drainages, giving rise to the Meadow Creek (Stibnite after 1928) and Yellow Pine Districts (Gold Hill in 1902, Morrison in 1904, and finally Yellow Pine in 1905). At Thunder Mountain, mining would be a war of attrition among the syndicates. Dewey Mining was the principle producer, the Belle of Thunder Mountain Co. (Belleco) was second, while the Pittsburgh Group would spend heavily but never produce. The Twentieth Century Mining and Power Company, the latecomer, arrived in 1905, and lasted until 1910.

At Thunder Mountain and at Buffalo Hump, the ores would prove rich on the surface, but the lode shallow and short-lived. The Pittsburgh Group in 1905, the Belleco in 1906, and finally the Dewey in 1907, preceded the

Twentieth Century in its demise. Even Roosevelt, then with a population of 35 would disappear in 1909. The once-proposed county seat of Mineral County would go dramatically. On May 31, 1905, a mudslide blocked Monumental Creek below town. The result is Roosevelt Lake, which drowned Roosevelt, the town.

Hoping for bigger profits to be gained from the gold rush, the Oregon Short Line dropped its backing of the Idaho Northern in 1901, and surveyed its own line from its Mackay Branch toward Thunder Mountain. When the boom fizzled in 1903, the OSL abandoned the project altogether. The Dewey Syndicate continued its efforts with the Idaho Northern and continued construction from Nampa, which had begun in 1899. It reached Emmett in 1902, and became stalled in a lawsuit over electric waterpower with another syndicate.

The old main wagon road from Boise to Long Valley was via Pearl, Ola, Sweet, and Tripod Lake to Smiths Ferry, then over Neebs Hill to Crawford and Van Wyck. From Crawford, a pack trail evolved to Knox, near Warm Lake, when the gold rush began. With his railroad stalled and the Dewey Mine needing large equipment, Dewey obtained public funding to rebuild that trail into a wagon road in 1902. The road was not completed until 1904, and even then Belleco paid for the last few miles.

This wagon road gained the name Thunder Mountain Road, and at a shortcut south of Crawford, there arose in 1904, a major relay point named Thunder City.

With all the syndicates and the town of Roosevelt gone, the district still had good mines that were held by individuals and partnerships until World War II.

Train 385, with engine 643, a 2-8-0. It left Nampa at 8:30 a.m. and reached Smiths Ferry at 3:00 p.m. The final destination was McCall, arriving at 6:15 p.m. H. A. Petersen Collection.

History of the Idaho Northern

The original owner of the Idaho Northern was Colonel W. H. Dewey, a mining nabob of Nampa. As chartered in 1897, the railroad was to run as far south as Paradise Valley, Nevada, as far north as Spokane, Washington, as far east as Butte, Montana, and as far west as the Willamette Valley of Oregon, via its sister railroad, the Oregon Eastern. Enroute, it would tap Dewey's mining interest at Thunder Mountain and Buffalo Hump. The Dewey Cartel held 119,994 of the 120,000 shares of stock issued and was merely the General Agent for the Union Pacific, which controlled over $14,000,000 of the bonds of the line.

Few today would guess that even though it is located in a remote corner of the west, the history of the Idaho

Northern is irrevocably interwoven with our national railroad history.

By 1901, James Jerome Hill, the empire Builder, had completed construction of the Great Northern and gained control of the Northern Pacific. He also controlled the Chicago & Northwestern and the Burlington. For all these railroads however, he had only one Pacific terminus, in Seattle, and he needed a direct line to San Francisco. In 1872, the Northern Pacific had found and surveyed a route to San Francisco via the Salmon River.

In 1898, Edward E. Harriman gained control of the Union Pacific. Under his management, the UP gained control of the Southern Pacific and standardized operations. One part of Harriman's objective was to prevent Hill from reaching San Francisco, which the Southern Pacific thoroughly controlled.

Finally, there was Jay Gould who controlled the Denver & Rio Grande and the Missouri Pacific, with his ambition to have his own system stretching from coast to coast. George, Jay's eldest son, who succeeded his father in 1892, decided to build a new road, the Western Pacific, to San Francisco. What he still wanted was a route to the Pacific Northwest, which was either through Idaho via the Salmon or through Oregon via the Deschutes River.

In 1898, Idaho's railroad law was in its infancy. When right-of-way was contested, whoever promised the most to the state/citizenry would win in court, which is where the proxies of these tycoons would spend the next dozen years. The way to the court's heart was to have local companies fronting the stock and the tycoons controlling the bonds which actually financed construction. The legal catch was that if a railroad was not built within three years of the claim, the route reverted to public domain.

By 1906, these tussles had reached comic proportions. The Union Pacific and the Chicago & Northwestern were slugging it out on the Payette River. The Illinois Central and Northern Pacific where both claiming ownership of the Clearwater Shortline and its successor, the Camas Prairie. Hill had $178,000,000 in backing to construct the Butte, Boise & San Francisco from Caldwell, Idaho, to Adrian, Oregon. The Burlington was surveying the south bank of the Snake River under its own name and the ' Denver, Yellowstone & Pacific was starting a line from Casper, Wyoming, to Boise, Idaho, as an extension of the Chicago & Northwestern.

In the middle of this wrangling was Dewey with his little Boise, Nampa & Owyhee, incorporated as a limited partnership, on February 7, 1896, which was destined to reach only as far as Murphy, Idaho. Harriman obviously had some influence on Dewey and the BN&O, as the Chief Engineer of the Oregon Short Line supervised the BN&O's construction.

The railroad war overtook the BN&O the following year, 1898, when it was made a subsidiary of the Idaho Northern with its pretentious goals of reaching Nevada, Montana, and Washington. Several interesting questions surround the Idaho Northern (IN) in these early years that probably will never be answered:
⇒ The IN was incorporated on December 18, 1897, as a subsidiary to the BN&O. Why did the BN&O become a subsidiary of the Idaho Northern one-year later?

49

⇒ What connection did Dewey, his Syndicate, and/or the Idaho Northern have with Hill? Soon after the IN's incorporation, Hill started construction of the Clearwater Shortline south from Lewiston. The IN reported its northern terminus as Lewiston, Idaho, although its maps indicate Spokane, Washington. The proposed IN line north was following Northern Pacific's surveys.

All indications are that, at the time of its incorporation the Idaho Northern was in the camp of Jerome Hill and by 1899, it was firmly under the control of Harriman and the Union Pacific.

The history of the Idaho Northern Board of Directors gives no indication of any outside influences. It consisted of local individuals and changed very little over the years. At the time of its incorporation it consisted of W. H. Dewey, E. H. Dewey, H. A. Partridge, R. M. Esteem, C. R. Hickey and A. I. Hede. When W. H. Dewey died in 1903, his son E. H. Dewey would move up to his place on all boards of Dewey holdings, and his younger brother, W. C. Dewey would take the place vacated by E. H. The board configuration, when the Idaho Northern finally reached Long Valley, would be E. H. Dewey, President and General Manager, W. C. Dewey, Vice President, A. J. Made, Secretary, and J. D. Bloomfield, Treasurer.

Initially there was no urgency to railroad construction other than completing the line to Murphy. It seems that the UP perceived the threat of Hill coming south as neutralized since the Idaho Northern was in Harriman's hands.

50

In 1899, however, the UP presumed that Hill had reappeared in an unlikely guise that would stall the Idaho Northern from progressing for years--as an electric power company. That year, H. K. Dunn announced that he represented a group of Boston Financiers who intended to build a power plant in Black Canyon, above Emmett. The only other name to come out of this mysterious group was a Mr. Noble, who later built the Boise Valley Railway, one of the two electric railroads out of Boise. Dunn proclaimed that when the power plant was completed, they would build an electric railroad from Emmett to Weiser and south to Silver City, parallel with the BN&O. Seeing Hill in this proclamation, the UP sprang into action and surveyed the Idaho Northern between Nampa and Emmett.

The danger of an electric power plant to a railroad at that time was the fact that a railroad was superseded in law by electric power--more public benefit--meaning that the railroad must route around anything held by a public utility, including the high water mark of a reservoir.

By August 18, 1899, the Idaho Northern surveyors were camped at the base of Freezeout Hill and had run the survey to Emmett, as far as Commercial Street. By September 15, they had reached the Black Canyon east of Emmett. On September 16, Dewey made a public plea for the residents of Emmett to donate land to expedite the grading of the railroad, especially 40 acres in the city center. Donations, however, were not forthcoming. Instead the railroad received $30,000 in claims against it for land taken.

In the meantime, Dunn and his power company seemed to have evaporated and Hill was back under the name of the

Idaho Midland, this time coming from a new direction, the Boise River.

At this point in time, the Dewey Syndicate was buying claims at Thunder Mountain and awarded a contract to J. J. McDonald to survey beyond Emmett for a new Dewey company, the Payette River Extension Railroad. Instead of surveying to Long Valley, the UP's preferred route, McDonald surveyed east at the Clear Creek over the summit to the South Fork of the Salmon, heading for Dewey's mining interests. On December 20, 1899, McDonald's survey died a legal death. On that date, an injunction was filed by Willard White, a local Emmett resident, against the railroad for violating Dunn's proposed dam-site. Shortly thereafter, in early 1900, the dam project was taken over by Union Light & Power of Utah. In consortium with Dunn's Boston backers, this company incorporated as the People's Electric Company, with a 20-year franchise to generate power and operate electric railroads. The Idaho Northern counter-sued on land ownership. However the wrangle would tie up any construction above Emmett until 1906.

Confident about the area south of Emmett, the railroad awarded a contract to Frazer & Chambers of Chicago to build a steel bridge over the Boise River near Middleton on December 22, 1899. On March 9, 1900, it also awarded contracts to J. H. Smith & Co. for gradework between Nampa and Emmett. Tracklaying did not begin until March 11, 1901, and the railroad finally crawled into Emmett on March 29, 1902. There it would languish until 1906, stalled because of the lawsuit mentioned earlier.

While the Idaho Northern was stalled at Emmett with the lawsuit, its claim north of Emmett had run out and the Chicago & Northwestern jumped in, filing right-of-way claims down the Salmon, the Boise, and the South Fork of the Payette River. At the same time, H. K. Dunn reappeared with $10,000 in bonds and the intention of blocking the line's western expansion from Emmett. He incorporated the Payette Valley Railroad--with the Chicago & Northwestern as bondholder--on February 3, 1906, and began construction from Emmett to New Plymouth.

Harriman and Hill had been tooth and nail over Hill's Oregon Grand Trunk railroad in Oregon and Hill's assault in Idaho seems to have caught Harriman off guard. The immediate reaction was for the Union Pacific to seize management of the Idaho Northern, a move allowed, as the line had never paid interest on its bonds. Meanwhile the UP started the Hell's Canyon Railroad (Homestead Branch) toward Lewiston to squash any notions Hill may have had for that route.

But Harriman ultimately solved the Hill problem in 1907, when he bought control of the Chicago & Northwestern. In 1909, Harriman died and a Federal Court decided that the UP had to buy out all Hill holdings in Idaho and Oregon, in whole or at least half. Through this, the Payette Valley and the Butte, Boise & San Francisco, as small as they were, came into the UP stable.

So sat the Idaho Northern at Emmett while the clock ran against the C&NW surveys. By the time the claim on the surveys had run out in 1910, Hill had regained control of the C&NW and it was war all over again. This time with a new player, a close personal friend of James Hill's, Frederick Weyerhaeuser. Weyerhaeuser owned huge tracts of timber on the Payette and the Boise River.

The Weyerhaeuser syndicates had spent large sums of money trying to drive logs on those rivers, and by 1910, it was obvious that they needed railroads in both locations. Hill backed the little Gilmore & Pittsburgh from Montana to Salmon, Idaho. From Salmon, the G&P resurveyed the same routes that the C&NW had done in 1906, in the name of the San Francisco Mailroute, and this time Weyerhaeuser surveyed out to meet them. The outcome on the Boise River was the Intermountain Railway, which would never connect with the G&P and was abandoned in the 1930s.

UP 284 on train #396 near Rainbow Bridge, December 31, 1947. H. A. Petersen Collection. H. R. Griffiths photo.

On the Payette and for the Idaho Northern, it was more of the same. The Union Pacific counterclaimed everything that the C&NW had claimed, but for the first time it intended to be rid of Hill once and for all and actually started spending money on the line. It completed the Payette Valley from New Plymouth to Payette on September 20, 1910. H. K. Dunn was kept as General Manager, W. L. McDonald of Chicago was brought in as Chief Engineer, and Fred Barnes as Superintendent. These two also received the same titles on the Idaho Northern.

On the disputed land in Black Canyon, the District Court ruled that the People's Electric Company, which had been absorbed into a conglomerate doing business as the Idaho Railway, Light & Power Company in 1909, did in fact own it. The first step, therefore, for the UP was a new survey, which took the railroad further--and more expensively--up the hillside. By August 11, 1910, the road had been surveyed to the Spink ranch, between Roseberry and McCall, and construction finally began in May, 1911.

Construction contracts were awarded to Utah Construction for general contracting, Wasatch Construction for subcontracting, and Brown & Packett for grading, all companies that the UP had used before. Tracklaying would be done by the railroad itself, hiring its own labor and using a Harris tracklaying machine. In all, 2,500 men were hired by the contractors and the railroad.

Yet despite this activity, only four miles of grading was completed in 1911. Resources kept being diverted elsewhere, for the Idaho Northern was only one piece of the colossus meant to lick Hill. But grading stalled for yet another reason. Once more the railroad was forced to abandon its proposed route in the "public interest." This time it was because of the Black Canyon Irrigation District, a new entity that was created after the surveys had been completed. A new line was resurveyed over the

55

winter and work started over from Emmett in February of 1912, on what is the current route.

Grading was finished to Banks by April of 1912, assisted by the Oregon Eastern, getting mired in mud during March, and its work force being released to help on the Idaho Northern. The holdup on tracklaying was ties. Long Valley had numerous sawyers, but collectively they could not keep up with the voracious appetite of the Harris machine.

Nevertheless, the railroad announced it would be running to Payette Lake by November 30 of 1912, but that proved to be optimistic. The rails reached Smiths Ferry on July 10, 1913. An inaugural special was scheduled from Nampa to Smiths Ferry for July 27, but that was delayed by bad weather until August 3. Regular service from Nampa to Smiths Ferry began on August 20.

The Idaho Northern was finally completed in early July of 1914, and regular service began on the 19th, running to McCall on Mondays, Wednesdays, and Fridays and back to Nampa on the days between. The trains were mixed – freight, express, mail, and passengers, and went to daily service in both directions by 1916.

Far short of its initial ambitions, the Idaho Northern would never extend beyond McCall. The war with Hill had ended enroute up the canyon, with Hill finishing the Seattle, Portland & Spokane, which gave him access to San Francisco in league with Gould's Western Pacific.

From 1916 through 1939, when Boise Payette Lumber moved its cutting operations from Payette to the Weiser River drainage, the primary commodities on the Branch

were Boise Payette sawlogs, and ties milled by Hoff &
Brown (later Brown Tie and Lumber) in McCall.

From 1940 to 1954, the primary commodities were
Brown ties and livestock. Boise Payette bought the
Cascade Mill from Halleck & Howard Lumber in 1953,
and the main lading was logs and lumber products until
2001.

In May of 1980, the Union Pacific abandoned the line
between Cascade and McCall and the connection between
Nampa and Emmett followed in 1996. What remained of
the Idaho Northern was sold by the Union Pacific in the
mid-1990s, to the Idaho Northern & Pacific. With the
closure of the Boise Cascade Mill in Horseshoe Bend in
1998, the only remaining customer on the line between
Emmett and Cascade is the Boise Cascade Mill in
Cascade.

Logging Railroads

Boise Payette Lumber operated a network of logging
railroads out of Cascade, including a line into Crawford
Nook that operated between 1916–1919. The company's
headquarters was relocated in 1919, from Cascade to
Cabarton, and a new line was constructed from there into
Round Valley. Additional lines were also constructed up
Clear Creek, Skunk Creek, and Big Creek in Long Valley.
When the Great Depression struck, Boise Payette ceased
logging in Long Valley, operating only in the Boise Basin
until it was cut out in 1934.

Boise Payette returned briefly to Long Valley in 1934,
building a line from Cascade to Van Wyck that year and
then moved up to MacGregor to cut on the Gold Fork.

57

This operation closed in 1939, when the company relocated to Council. In 1953, Boise Payette bought the Halleck & Howard mill at Cascade, and renewed logging in Long Valley. By now, however, trucks had replaced logging railroads.

Dion Lumber opened in 1924, in Cascade, but through a series of sales the mill became W. H. Eccles Lumber in 1926. Eccles relocated from Oregon, bringing the company's narrow gauge railroad. This 3-foot gauge operated on Pearsol and Beaver Creeks. In 1928, Eccles was sold to Denver-based Halleck & Howard Lumber, which closed the mill and railroad during the Depression. After 1933, the railroad operated only a short time before trucks took over. The Halleck & Howard (nee Eccles) locomotive #3 remained on the property as an auxiliary boiler. It remained in this use after Boise Payette bought the Cascade Mill from Halleck & Howard. In 1974, the locomotive was purchased by Sumpter Valley Railroad Preservation, and is still used as a tourist locomotive at McEwen, Oregon.

Flora & Fauna

The Payette River is abundant in wildlife and passengers frequently have the opportunity of sighting a variety of animals along the river. Following is a short list of the flora and fauna that may be seen along the line (list provided by the Idaho Department of Fish & Game-- species represent known occurrences in the general area, but does not represent potential or consistent distribution):

- **Mammals**: moose, elk, deer, otters, mink, beaver, red fox, black bear, mountain lion, wolverine, fisher, squirrels.

- **Amphibians/Reptiles**: Long-toed salamander, Idaho giant salamander, western toad, spotted frog, western chorus frog, tailed frog, northern leopard frog, sagebrush lizard, side-blotched lizard, rubber boa, gopher snake, western garter snake, western rattlesnake.

- **Fish:** bull trout, inland Columbia Basin redband trout.

- **Large birds**: American crow, bald eagle, belted kingfisher, black-billed magpie, black-crowned night heron, Cooper's hawk, double-crested cormorant, forest grouse, green-horned owl, golden eagle, great-blue heron, great gray owl, gull, northern goshawk, osprey, peregrine falcon, red-tailed hawk, ring-necked pheasant, ruffed grouse, sandhill crane, turkey vulture, western screech-owl, white pelican.

- **Small birds**: American pipit, black-backed woodpecker, boreal owl, cedar waxwing, flammulated owl, lazuli bunting, Lewis woodpecker, mountain bluebird, mountain quail, northern pygmy owl, pygmy nuthatch, robin, ruby-throated hummingbird, three-toed woodpecker, tree swallow, upland sandpiper, western tanager.

- **Waterfowl**: bufflehead, Canada goose, common merganzer, gadwall, green-winged teal, mallard, western grebe.

- **Water/shore birds**: American avocet, American dipper, black-necked stilt, common loon, long-billed dowitcher, killdeer, kingfisher, red-necked grebe, water ouzel, western grebe, western sandpiper.

- **Plants**: bitterbrush, bank monkeyflower, bulb-bearing waterhemlock, crested wheatgrass, Idaho bitterroot, lemon grass, medusa head wild rye native bunchgrass, pod grass, poison ivy, rush aster, sagebrush, slick spot peppergrass, swamp onion, syringa, wolf's currant.

- **Trees**: douglas fir, Engleman spruce, grand fir, hackberry, lodgepole pine, ponderosa pine, western larch, willow, cottonwood.

Historical Vignettes

Memories of A. A. Storkman and E. G. Nydegger (1963 newspaper article, paper unknown, "Railroaders Tell of Incidents in Early Days on McCall Run," by Annie Laurie Bird), as provided by Elizabeth Cuff:

"The first Sunday in August, 1913, 68 persons from Nampa, 16 from Caldwell, 17 from Meridian and 52 from Emmett joined a group from the Payette Valley for an excursion of the new Idaho Northern to Smiths Ferry.

"This trip up the picturesque Payette River, with its canyons, cataracts and broad reaches of water, is one of the most scenic in the state. The good fishing, the ideal surroundings with lofty mountains rising from the river's edge and covered with timber, and the altitude such as to insure coolness combined to make the excursion a fascinating one. Many were said to be awestricken with

60

the grandeur of the scenery, the beautiful gorges and the canyons.

"By the last of September, the track was within 18 miles of the terminus at Payette Lakes. Two months later train service was established to Cascade and two-story depots had been built at Montour, Horseshoe Bend, Banks, Smiths Ferry and Cascade.

"Heavy rock and dirt slides five miles from Banks caused trouble in January, 1914, as did slides later above Horseshoe Bend. Yet on June 26, 1914, President A. L. Mohler of the Union Pacific, likewise president of the Oregon Short Line, spent Tuesday night at Lakeport, new name of the town of McCall, Payette Lakes terminal of the Idaho Northern.

"Track laying had been completed to that point and regular service was to be inaugurated the middle of July. The daily schedule announced a train was to leave Nampa at 2:25 p.m. and arrive at Lakeport at 9:05 p.m. The train from Lakeport would leave at 7 a.m. and arrive at Nampa at 1:30 p.m.

"This news was welcomed by the many Nampans who vacationed each year either at Payette Lakes or along the Payette River. Surely the train trip would be a more comfortable means of reaching their destination than the time consuming, hot and dusty journey by horse and buggy over the narrow, winding roads, or even by automobile whose radiator had a way of boiling on the steepest pitches--always, seemingly, where descent to the river to obtain water needed to cool it was most difficult-- and where, if vehicles going the opposite direction were not seen in time, the car must back down around curves

61

until a turn-out was reached so the two vehicles could pass with some degree of safety.

"Mr. Nydegger began his work as a fireman on September 19, 1913, and had the pleasure of firing on the first mixed train into Cascade. As the track was completed, the run was lengthened, and other 'first trains' for which he fired were those into Arling (now under the waters of Lake Cascade), Donnelly and McCall itself.

"Snow slides, fires and derailments were oft recurring dangers on the line and the crews were constantly on the alert for signs of them. In 1917, the snow was so deep that he was on the work train for 30 days before it was able to reach McCall. The bridge gang had to shovel a portion of some drifts before the rotary, pushed by four engines, could go in to clear the track.

"The train was so long in making the trip from Smiths Ferry to Cascade that people had to snowshoe to the train itself for supplies or else starve. It was bringing up eight cars of merchandise, supplies and food for stores along the route, and these kept the inhabitants of Crockett *(Author's note: Crawford perhaps)* and Van Wyck in needed food and supplies until another train could get through.

"The crews had some fun along with clearing the track. They would take scoop shovels to the top of the hills, get on them and slide down the slopes, scooting clear across the frozen river.

"Another snow episode Mr. Nydegger remembers was when a large number of people were on the train, bound for a dance at Cabarton. Halfway between Smiths Ferry and Cabarton, a snow slide hit the train, almost burying it.

The passengers got out, seized shovels and helped dig out the engine. Then the rest of the train was uncoupled from the engine, all the people got on it and away to the dance!

"Mr. Storkman, who served first as a brakeman, then as a conductor on the Idaho Northern, recalls that from the time the Idaho Northern was built until he retired there always were snow storms on February 7 and 14. One time he was riding in the engine when it was hit by a snow slide so high and so heavy that the front of the engine was lifted off the track and by the time it was stopped, was headed for the river. The train was often snowed-in until slides could be removed, one time from 10:30 a.m. until 4 a.m. the following day.

"Rock slides were frequent and often damaging on the Idaho Northern. During the depression years they were nicknamed 'Pennies From Heaven,' since their removal provided the extra work much desired at that time. A rock from one slide landed in an empty coal car, bent up both ends and derailed it. The crew, who had to be experts in getting derailed cars back on the tracks, rerailed this damaged car as best as they could, then chained it to the car in front and the engine dragged it and the fore part of the train to the nearest side-track, then returned for the balance of the train and continued the trip.

"When a slide hit the side-rod of the engine and disabled the mechanism, the train had to wait until the wrecker arrived and towed the useless engine to Nampa for repairs. Such was the case when a guard rail on a bridge across the Payette River became loosened and pierced the water tank behind the engine. Since the engine could not operate without water, it remained there on the bridge all night until another engine arrived to take it to Nampa.

"An unusual fact about this delay was that Superintendent Manson's private car was attached to this particular train. When Mr. Nydegger was questioned as to whether this delay caused his being demoted or fired, he answered, 'No, I was promoted!'

"Initiative in crisis seemed to be a prime requisite for crews on the Idaho Northern. Passengers and people along the line often wondered 'if the crew had gone fishing,' as they did not realize that the maximum speed was 25 miles an hour and on many portions was only 10 miles per hour.

"Throughout the summer months, fire patrols followed each train to put out fires started by sparks or tiny cinders that had penetrated the 'boohoos' with which all engines where equipped so that cinders would be kept from flying. Even with such precautions, fires sometimes broke out.

"Such was the case in the 'big fire.' Mr. Storkman was on a stock train bound for McCall, and the fire patrol, as was their duty, followed the train. 'My engines,' said Mr. Storkman, 'were numbers 513, 523 and 613, and my caboose was 613.' A spark from one of them was said to have caused the fire. Although the patrol discovered the fire within three or four minutes after it started, they were unable to put it out. The damage caused was estimated at some $60,000 since it burned from Banks to Hank Goul's camp on both sides of the road.

"Mr. Nydegger had an experience he will never forget with that fire. He had just transferred back to the Idaho Northern after months as an engineer on the main line, and this was his first trip to McCall after the transfer. When the mixed train reached the fire zone, he and his foreman, Charles Wilson, decided their engine could make it through safely and outrun the fire.

"When they reached the bridge across the river, some ties were on fire. The train stopped and the crew put these out, then started on to Mains, three miles above. The fire, however, turned, came back over the hill and was so hot that he opened the blow-off valves of the engine and thus permitted the train to get through safely. This took practically all the water in the boiler and when the train reached Mains ahead of the fire, it was stopped to permit Mr. Nydegger and Mr. Wilson to fill the boiler from the water tank back of the engine. Helper engine number 523, the one blamed for setting the fire, was on the Mains' siding, on its way back from McCall.

"While the boiler was filling, the crew discovered a sheep car on fire and all rushed for buckets to put this out, leaving one injector valve open to fill the boiler. As a result, steam was too low to operate the engine and the fire caught up with the train. Engine 523 was hooked on in front of the train's engine and the trip to Big Eddy was made. Cab windows were cracked by the intense heat as burning timber roared like a lion. The fire had crossed to the other side of the river at the bridge and was on both sides of the river, as the train raced to safety.

"Throughout the whole episode, a woman passenger in the coach had crocheted calmly. She said she was not afraid. When the fire had turned back, the patrol saved themselves by lying down in the river and waiting there until the danger had passed."

Picket's Corral, as provided by Evelyn Harper:

"This could be called the story of Picket's Corral or the story of the Payette Vigilantes and their illustrious captain. In the spring of 1863, the Boise Basin gold discovery exploded on to the world. Placerville, Centerville, Pioneerville, Quartzburg, and Idaho City (then known as Bannock), were located in the center of that gold rush. A young man, Willima J. McConnel, raised in Michigan, at 21 years of age started west in 1860, to follow the excitement. In California, he discovered that the man who raised vegetables in the neighborhood of those gold mines did a far better job financially than those who hunted for gold. McConnel came to the Boise area, found a sunny location in the Jerusalem Valley on Jerusalem Creek above Horseshoe Bend, and went to work raising vegetables. He started by planting two bushels of onions. In about a month's time he sold 100 bunches of onions at $1.00 a bunch in Placerville; the first green vegetables sold in the Boise Basin. His endeavors were a great success and he gradually branched out and sold all kinds of vegetables just as quickly as he could plant and harvest.

"Wherever there is gold there are also thieves trying to reap the rewards of someone else's hard labor. Thieves robbed, murdered, passed bogus gold, and stole horses, mules, and cows. Local government in and around the mining camps was undeveloped and there was no militia to protect the property and lives of those who lived in the area. Three men who had been engaged in robbing stages and stealing horses and cattle in New Mexico, came to Idaho in 1863. The area was ripe for plunder. After bringing the miners west, thousands of mules and horses had been turned loose near Horseshoe Bend to feed on the lush grass. The thieves would round up a herd of animals at night and drive them to Oregon, Nevada or California, and sell them for a very profitable sum. For the return trip they would rob and plunder that area and return with horses and mules to sell to the Idaho people who had their horses robbed. These three men headquartered in the Emmett Valley near the entrance to the canyon leading to Horseshoe Bend. They called their headquarters Picket's Corral and they built a log house and a corral strong enough to act as a fort. It was built in front of a natural cave of rocks in the canyon wall. The cabin was built out of driftwood and was a stopping place for travelers and freighters on their way to Horseshoe Bend. It was the last watering place until you came out of the canyon at the Marsh-Ireton Ranch, also a stopover inn near Montour. The Picket's Corral Gang became the most notorious outlaws in southern Idaho.

"The thieves built a second ranch in what is now the south part of Boise. They had a lookout tower just east of where the Broadway Bridge now crosses the Boise River. The buildings were hidden from view down in the thick willows and cottonwoods next to the river. Here they would also hold stolen animals for a few days before heading out to sell them. Because they were big, good looking men, fine horsemen, and generous to those in trouble, they found it easy to work their way into local politics. One of their members, Dave Updyke, was elected sheriff of Ada County, which was an added protection to their thievery.

"At this time Bill McConnel was raising vegetables and hauling them into the Boise Basin, making money beyond his fondest dreams. But he lost it almost as fast when the thieves made raids on his livestock. One day, when his favorite saddle horse was missing, he rode down to Boise City and searched the livery stables. He didn't find his favorite mare but found some horses that had been stolen months before. McConnell and a young lawyer friend, who had just started practice, decided to seek justice in the court. But the thieves were in control and McConnell ended up paying a back livery bill that was more than the value of the horses he found. Right then and there he decided to take justice into his own hands. The thieves decided to teach the "rutahaga peddler" a thing or two. A few nights later they raided Jerusalem Valley, stealing five valuable horses and four large mules worth $2,000. McConnell gathered a posse of four gardeners from the valley and started after the thieves. They caught them at camp in the middle of the night near LaGrande, Oregon, and after a fight they ended up bringing their horses and mules back home.

"At this the ranchers in the Payette Valley decided to form an organized group to protect their property and their lives. Thus the Payette Vigilante Committee was organized. McConnell was elected captain. Their rules were simple. An accused man was entitled to a trial by jury of seven members of the Committee. A majority vote would render a verdict. For conviction there were three kinds of sentences: leave the country within 24 hours, be publicly horsewhipped, or be hanged. The story is told that while the Vigilante Committee was meeting in the second story of the Block House, the thieves stole into the first floor and ate their meal which was simmering over the fireplace, leaving the dirty dishes and no food for those citizens seriously meeting above them.

"As their first project, the Committee decided to clear out counterfeiters who were passing bogus gold. In San Francisco, lead bars were cut into tiny particles and galvanized with real gold. It was difficult to distinguish the bogus gold from the real gold. Headquarters for the bogus gold syndicate was with the Picket's Corral Gang. Miners passing through the area and staying at the Inn for the night would leave their real gold in the Inn's safe for safekeeping and receive the bogus gold when they picked up their gold the next morning. The Committee voted to serve Conklin, the bogus gold agent, with notice to leave the country within 24 hours. A group of six Committee members was chosen to serve the notice, and one of the six was elected as leader. The leader went into the Picket's Corral bar and overheard Conklin and three outlaws planning to kill him after luring him outside. But he pulled out his two revolvers and said he would make them the biggest funeral in the Payette Valley. When the rest of his committee joined him, the thieves made no effort to defend themselves and listened as the vigilantes read the 24-hour verdict. In the end the bogus gold agent left the country and the syndicate called off its operations in the area. This success of the committee worried the outlaws.

"There were two brothers who owned the Washoe Ferry on the Oregon side of the Snake River near Payette, and they were well known for harboring criminals. They issued a challenge to the Payette Vigilantes to try to take the ferry house. The house was practically a fort with no windows, only gun holes, and a dirt roof that could not be set afire. The Vigilante Committee decided to take up the challenge. Twenty men rode out through a foot of snow leaving 16 men near the ferry on the Idaho side. They sent in one man, who was unknown to the brothers, as a traveler wanting to get across the river. Since he seemed to be a stranger, the brothers let him in and he immediately headed to the fireplace to pile a bunch of sagebrush onto the fire, causing a burst of smoke to come out of the chimney, thus alerting the remaining members of his group as to his success in gaining entrance. They immediately rushed in and took over the ferry house. The sleeping men didn't have a chance. The Committee met and sentenced the brothers to banishment from the territory.

"The outlaws in the area became very alarmed and Sherriff Updyke, in Ada County, issued warrants for the arrest of the Vigilantes, spreading the word that they were a bunch of cutthroats. They especially wanted Captain McConnell. But a friend of McConnell's rode through the snow to warn McConnell and the captain decided to ride down to meet them. A party of five took off down the Payette River. The deputies stopped at the stage station, and as the five approached the station they saw a row of guns propped against the outside wall of the building. Before Picket's Corral men could be forewarned, the five Vigilantes opened the door and humiliated the thieves by pulling guns on them. Because the Sheriff had no evidence against McConnell and the Vigilantes, warrants against them were dropped. Sheriff Updyke later resigned from his position.

"Bill McConnell went on to become U.S. Marshall, cattleman, merchant, delegate to the National Republican Convention, President of the Oregon State Senate, member of the Idaho Constitution Convention, Idaho's first U.S. Senator after statehood, Governor of Idaho for two terms, Indian Inspector, Immigration Inspector, and historian."

Acknowledgements

This book would not have been possible without the help of many people. My gratitude goes to:

- Jim Witherell, who provided historical information.
- H. A. Petersen, for providing most of the photos.
- Chuck Wolfkiel, who provided the histories of Gardena and Horseshoe Bend.
- John Lawler of Idaho Whitewater Unlimited, who provided information on the Payette River.
- Wendy Miller, Curator of the Canyon County Historical Society Museum, who provided photos and information on W. H. Dewey.
- Joni Leipf, my wife, for proof reading the manuscript.

Bibliography

Boone, Lalia. *Idaho Place Names*. Moscow, Idaho: University of Idaho Press, 1988.

Conley, Cort. *Idaho for the Curious*. Cambridge, Idaho: Backeddy Books, 1982.

Huntley, James. *Ferry Boats in Idaho*. Caldwell, Idaho: Caxton Printers, 1979.

Idaho Transportation Department. *Idaho Bridge Inventory*. Boise, Idaho: 1983

Kent, Brian and Kent, John. *The Journal of George E. H. Faull*. Kent, 1999.

Rudolph, Teresa, Editor. *The Hetrick Site*. Boise, Idaho: Idaho Transportation Department, 1995.

Stuebner, Stephen. Paddling the Payette. Trade Paperback, 1996.

Witherell, Jim. *The Log Trains of Southern Idaho*. Denver, Colorado: Sundance Publications, 1989.

Trip Notes

Trip Notes

Trip Notes